HOW TO
GET THE JOB

**31 Lessons for
the Entry-Level
Job Seeker**

Author – Todd Aten

Published in Brownsville, Texas by Todd Aten

Cover design and interior artwork by Hope Barnard
On A Whim Designs

ISBN-13: 9781703719390

> # FOR OVER TWENTY YEARS, I HAVE SAID: "I WISH I COULD TEACH A CLASS ON HOW TO GET A JOB."

INTRODUCTION

I've heard it said that everyone has worked at either McDonald's or Pizza Hut at some point in their lives. I did, and I know that it is true for a lot of people. You have to start working somewhere and restaurants, grocery stores and the like often provide the kind of opportunities that we need; especially, when we are just starting out.

Teachers, friends and the people who did "Career Day" may have told you things like "you need to make an application and have a resume", but nobody tells you much more than that. You then, head out into uncharted waters and hope for the best, unaware that you may be sabotaging yourself. It's frustrating, discouraging and often leads to a sense of hopelessness and foreboding.

For over twenty years, I have said: "I wish I could teach a class on how to get a job." It's a thought that has never gone away and, with my recent return to the role of hiring manager, it seems more necessary now than ever. So many people, young and old, are lacking basic knowledge, understanding and insight into the job-search process and it's killing their job opportunities.

I am a manager and a seasoned journeyman. From the age of sixteen, I have worked my way up through the ranks. I've worked in sales and a lot in the food service industry. I have interviewed and hired countless people in a span of over thirty years. In short, I'm the guy who will decide if you get the job, so I thought it might be helpful for you to see through my eyes.

About ninety percent of what will get you the job lies in what you do before you ever leave your house. A few simple "do's and don'ts" can make or break your chances of getting hired. With simple, yet powerful lessons, along with thought-provoking questions, this workbook is designed to help you think about things that you may have never thought about and were definitely never taught.

> ## "ABOUT NINETY PERCENT OF WHAT WILL GET YOU THE JOB LIES IN WHAT YOU DO BEFORE YOU EVER LEAVE YOUR HOUSE."

KEY LESSONS

1 Make a great first impression

2 Be Prepared

3 Smile

4 Minimum wage is temporary

5 Scout your employer

6 Apply in person

7 Scrutiny begins immediately

8 Tatoos can limit opportunities

9 Use a full-length mirror

10 The dictionary is your friend

11 Your facebook page just cost you an interview

12 Resumes are supposed to look perfect

13 If you dont have a resume write a letter

14 I don't hire resumes or applications

15 Everything is a test — EVERYTHING

16 Punctuality is paramount

17 A good, firm handshake speaks volumes

18 I'm hiring based on MY needs

19 Why should I hire you?

20 When you're waiting in the lobby

21 Everybody has manners — good or bad

22 Your body language is loud

23 What is your job history?

24 Avoid using profanity

25 Prepare some good questions

26 Making eye contact

27 Entry level jobs are different from career jobs

28 Everyone has a website

29 Some hiring managers suck at interviewing

30 You are selling yourself

31 Small details are often the most important

DEDICATION

This book is dedicated to my mom and dad who raised me to be the man that I am today. My best qualities come from them while my worst are self-made. And, to my wife, Leigh. Your unwavering love and support both humbles and sustains me.

1

YOU NEVER GET A SECOND CHANCE TO MAKE A FIRST IMPRESSION

There's not a lot more to add to this old saying, other than that it is a fundamental truth in job seeking and in life. Everything else you learn should rest on this foundation.

It's also worth mentioning here that a poor second or third impression can easily wipe out your first one - no matter how good it was. Be aware, be intentional and be consistent!

> "BE AWARE, BE INTENTIONAL AND BE CONSISTENT!"

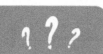

AFTER YOU HAVE READ THE ENTIRE BOOK, COME BACK AND ANSWER THE FOLLOWING QUESTIONS:

1. WHAT THINGS CAN I DO TO MAKE A GREAT FIRST IMPRESSION?

_____

_____

_____

_____

2. WHAT THINGS HAVE I DONE IN THE PAST TO HURT MY FIRST IMPRESSION?

_____

_____

_____

_____

2

THERE IS NO SUBSTITUTION FOR PREPAREDNESS

You may not have been a Boy Scout, but their motto: "Be Prepared" applies to everyone. When you come in to fill out an application, then ask to borrow a pen, I immediately question your level of preparation for every task that you will ever have. Unfair? Maybe, or maybe you should bring a pen with you!

Be prepared for some small talk or even the on-the-spot interview! You may be asked a few simple questions like: "What days and times are you available to work?" "What will be your transportation to and from work?" "Are you looking for full time or part time?" "How soon can you begin?"

Have your answers ready and be specific. I'm not just making conversation. I'm asking because I want to know. If you act caught off-guard and give me a flip, non-specific response then I think that you haven't really thought this whole "I need a job" thing through. You can never be too prepared, and the person most prepared is going to get the job.

> **"YOU CAN NEVER BE TOO PREPARED, AND THE PERSON MOST PREPARED IS GOING TO GET THE JOB."**

1. WHAT DAYS AND TIMES AM I AVAILABLE TO WORK?

_____

_____

2. HOW MANY HOURS PER WEEK DO I WANT/NEED TO WORK?

_____

_____

3. HOW SOON CAN I START?

_____

_____

3

IF YOU'RE NOT SMILING, YOU MIGHT WANT TO TRY GOVERNMENT WORK

When seeking a customer service job, never underestimate the power of a smile. The only time that a warm, authentic smile will not help you get the job is if the person or business doesn't value it. If that is the case, RUN! You probably don't want to work there.

If you are not the smiley type, you will be at a disadvantage when applying for jobs where you will be working directly with customers. You may be better suited for work that is less interactive with people; stock person, merchandising, guard work, etc. Understanding your strengths and weaknesses will help you to focus your job search efforts and find a fit that is better for both you and your employer.

> "UNDERSTANDING YOUR STRENGTHS AND WEAKNESSES WILL HELP YOU TO FOCUS YOUR JOB SEARCH EFFORTS."

1. DO I PREFER WORKING AROUND MORE PEOPLE (CUSTOMERS AND CO-WORKERS) OR FEWER PEOPLE?

_____

_____

2. WHAT COMPANIES AND EMPLOYERS OFFER JOBS THAT ARE MOST COMPATIBLE WITH MY PERSONALITY, STYLE AND PREFERENCE?

_____

_____

3. CAN I COMFORTABLY AND CONSISTENTLY "RISE TO THE OCCASION" TO MEET THE JOB REQUIREMENTS?

_____

_____

4

MINIMUM WAGE IS TEMPORARY, EXCEPT WHERE MINIMUM PERFORMANCE IS PERMANENT.

This is an entry level job; therefore, it will have entry level pay. You can build your value only after you get the job. Focusing on how little it pays is to miss the bigger picture. This is the job; this is what it pays and you have to start somewhere. You will not start higher until you have earned that right and are doing a job that has more value to your employer. The more valuable you become, the more you will earn.

Pay isn't everything. Many companies offer benefits like flexible scheduling, employee meals, discounts and even scholarships. Also, if you're new to the world of work, these employers are taking on the task of teaching you a trade and skills that you may use for the rest of your life – paying you while they build your value, so show a little respect.

Finally, remember that for the vast majority, this is a temporary job - not permanent, not a career. It's here for this season of your life. Remembering this perspective will help you with whatever deficiencies or other issues that you may have with the job.

> ## "THE MORE VALUABLE YOU BECOME, THE MORE YOU WILL EARN"

1. HOW CAN I PHRASE MY QUESTIONS ABOUT PAY AND BENEFITS TO GET THE INFORMATION WITHOUT SOUNDING PRESUMPTUOUS AND SELF-SERVING?

_____

_____

_____

2. HOW WILL I SHOW THE PERSON INTERVIEWING ME THAT I AM WILLING TO START AT THE BOTTOM AND EARN MY WAY UP?

_____

_____

_____

5

SCOUT YOUR POTENTIAL EMPLOYER TO SEE IF YOU FIT IN AND IF YOU REALLY WANT TO WORK THERE

If you are thinking of applying in a retail, food service or other "open to the public" business, stop by and visit before applying. Maybe you've been there before and have thought that it would be a good place to work, but have you really watched and observed the operation? Fifteen minutes of focused observation of employees, customers, bosses, etc. may help you determine if you will fit in and if it's really the kind of job that you want. It may also give you some valuable talking points that could help you in an interview.

> "FIFTEEN MINUTES OF FOCUSED OBSERVATION OF EMPLOYEES, CUSTOMERS, BOSSES, ETC. MAY HELP YOU DETERMINE IF YOU WILL FIT IN"

1. WHAT THINGS ARE IMPORTANT FOR ME TO HAVE IN A WORK ENVIRONMENT?

_____

_____

_____

2. WHAT THINGS IN THE WORK ENVIRONMENT WOULD BE A "DEAL-BREAKER" FOR ME?

_____

_____

_____

6

APPLY ONLINE IF YOU MUST, BUT IF YOU WILL STOP BY, INTRODUCE YOURSELF AND TELL ME THAT YOU HAVE APPLIED, YOU MAY MOVE TO THE TOP OF MY LIST

Here's the deal. Everything is moving to online. I get it. That doesn't mean that it's a good method for job application. Unless there are some real specifics in play, you are not really applying - you're entering your name in an online lottery where the odds are wildly against you.

Sadly, many fine companies subscribe to these methods and force you to play the game. You can't change that. What you can do is visit the place where you want to work. Find out who is in charge of hiring. Find out the best time to meet them. Set an appointment if necessary, but keep it casual. This takes just one or two minutes. Look them in the eye, shake their hand, tell them your name, that you applied online and that you are really interested in working there.

Congratulations! You've just done something that 99% of the other people didn't and won't, do. If you have followed the other advice and made a good first impression, you may now be at the top of the list. Don't be surprised if they want to set up an interview immediately.

As a side note, I'm not a big fan of the application follow-up call or unannounced visit. Generally, if you made a quality first impression, I'm going to give you an honest and clear expectation about what's next, so, your follow-up call is unnecessary. However, if when we met you asked something like: "If I don't hear from you, would it be okay to check back with you in about a week? When is the best day and time to do that?", I would have some respect for that.

Thoughtful, professional perseverance is a good thing as long as you don't come across as aggressive or desperate. Annoying me isn't going to help your cause.

1. AM I GOING ABOVE AND BEYOND IN MY EFFORTS OR AM I DOING THE BARE MINIMUM AND HOPING FOR THE BEST?

_____

_____

2. WHAT OTHER THINGS CAN I DO TO MAKE A POSITIVE, MEMORABLE IMPRESSION WITH THE PERSON IN CHARGE OF HIRING?

_____

_____

7

THE SCRUTINY BEGINS THE MOMENT YOU WALK THROUGH THE DOOR. I WILL OFTEN DECIDE IN LESS THAN A MINUTE WHETHER OR NOT I WANT TO CONSIDER YOU FURTHER BASED ON HOW YOU HAVE CHOSEN TO PRESENT YOURSELF

I cannot tell you how many times people show up with no thought to their appearance or conduct; like it's an afterthought on their way to the mall. I recently had someone come to the drive through to inquire about the job opening. They didn't even buy anything. If you can't even get out of your car, then you can't work for me.

If you really want a job, act like it! Be ready any time and every time you are anywhere near your prospective employer. You should be well-groomed, neatly and appropriately dressed with good hygiene and a respectful attitude.

"IF YOU REALLY WANT A JOB, ACT LIKE IT!"

1. WHAT WILL I WEAR WHEN I GO TO APPLY?

_____

_____

2. WHAT WILL I WEAR WHEN I GO TO AN INTERVIEW?

_____

_____

3. WHAT SHOULD I NEVER WEAR OR DO IN THE PRESENCE OF A PROSPECTIVE EMPLOYER?

_____

_____

8

FACT: PIERCINGS, TATTOOS AND OTHER VISIBLE EXPRESSIONS OF YOUR PERSONALITY WILL LIMIT YOUR OPPORTUNITIES

This may be unpopular or even offensive, but it is the absolute truth. America is great. Be who you want to be. Just understand that an employer wants someone who will blend in. They will not hire someone who clashes with their image or culture. If you've scouted the place and there are no man buns, tattoos, piercings, green hair, etc. Take the hint. They're not going to hire you, and your skills and other qualifications won't change that. There are places where these types of personality expressions are embraced. Your opportunities will be limited to those places.

If you already have any of the aforementioned, you should address it head on. Don't try to hide it with hats, turtlenecks and long sleeves. Ask if it is an issue and offer whatever remedies you are willing to make to meet their requirements. Questions like "Do I need to cut my hair to work here?" show self-awareness and respect. Discussing your tattoos out of concern for the employer may also provide you with an extra measure of grace. Again, respect...

> ## "QUESTIONS LIKE 'DO I NEED TO CUT MY HAIR TO WORK HERE?' SHOW SELF-AWARENESS AND RESPECT."

21

1. WHAT CHANGES AM I WILLING TO MAKE IN MY STYLE, FASHION AND GROOMING TO COMPLY WITH AN EMPLOYER'S CULTURE AND STANDARDS?

_____

_____

2. WHAT CHANGES AM I UNWILLING TO MAKE?

_____

_____

3. WHAT EMPLOYERS OFFER POSITIONS THAT BEST FIT MY STYLE AND PERSONALITY?

_____

_____

9

PROPER USE OF A FULL-LENGTH MIRROR WILL GREATLY IMPROVE YOUR CHANCES IN AN INTERVIEW

Appearance, appearance, appearance! Are you neatly and appropriately dressed? Is your shirt tucked in? If you've eaten recently, check your teeth and maybe chomp a breath mint! Do a final mirror check before you meet face to face and you may avoid a costly or embarrassing mistake.

Also, if you have six whiskers on your chin and only need to shave once a month, fine, but shave them off before you come see me.

If you wear a beard, trim it neatly and for Pete's sake, shave your neck! Because even if beards are allowed - and you should ask; that nasty looking rats nest of a thing on your face isn't!

"DO A FINAL MIRROR CHECK BEFORE YOU MEET FACE TO FACE"

1. AS I ASK OTHERS ABOUT MY APPEARANCE, WHAT DO THEY SAY?

_____

_____

_____

2. IF I HAD A CHECKLIST FOR A CLEAN AND PROFESSIONAL APPEARANCE, WHAT THINGS WOULD BE ON IT?

_____

_____

_____

10

THE DICTIONARY IS YOUR FRIEND APPLY - VERB. "GIVING ONE'S FULL ATTENTION TO A TASK, WORKING HARD"

I'm a fan of the sports term: "get your head in the game" and I will often look up words that I may already know the meaning of to do just that. Synonyms, antonyms, examples and word origins often give me new insight that can bring clarity and focus to the task at hand. Mental preparation will always serve you well.

If you think that applying for a job is just filling out a form, you may limit your efforts to that task and you might be missing some opportunities to shine. You're trying to get a job, so look up words like: apply, qualified, experience, work, job, interview, etc. You may find words, definitions and ideas that will help you.

Try this exercise and look for other creative ways to program your mind for success. Your brain is your best asset and Merriam-Webster is your friend. You will benefit by using both of them regularly.

> ## "IF YOU THINK THAT APPLYING FOR A JOB IS JUST FILLING OUT A FORM, YOU MAY LIMIT YOUR EFFORTS AND MISS AN OPPORTUNITY TO SHINE"

1. AFTER LOOKING UP THE FORMAL DEFINITION OF THE WORDS: "APPLY; QUALIFIED; EXPERIENCE; WORK; JOB AND INTERVIEW," HAS YOUR UNDERSTANDING OF THESE WORDS INCREASED? IF SO, HOW CAN YOU USE THIS BROADER UNDERSTANDING TO BENEFIT YOU IN YOUR JOB-SEARCH EFFORTS?

_____

_____

_____

_____

11

YOUR FACEBOOK PAGE JUST COST YOU A JOB INTERVIEW

Oh, so you applied online? Great! Since I'm already online, I think I'll check out your social media.

Your social media may be for your family and friends, but if it's open to public view, anything there can and will be used by a prospective employer. Inappropriate humor and pictures along with strong political or social views will absolutely have a negative impact on you with an employer. While I'm at it, a thousand lip-pursed selfies in sexy poses isn't going help your cause either.

If you must have your social media, be smart and use a pseudo name and/or, block it from public view. Employers are tech savvy and looking for information anywhere they can find it. Ignore this at your own peril. It's a silent job opportunity killer, and you will never know how much it will cost you.

> **"EMPLOYERS ARE TECH SAVVY AND LOOKING FOR INFORMATION ANYWHERE THEY CAN FIND IT"**

1. IS THERE ANYTHING ON MY SOCIAL MEDIA THAT COULD VIEWED NEGATIVELY BY A PROSPECTIVE EMPLOYER?

_____

_____

_____

12

RESUMES ARE SUPPOSED TO LOOK PERFECT. TYPOS, MISSPELLINGS AND POOR GRAMMAR ARE OPPORTUNITY KILLERS

For many entry level jobs, a resume may not be necessary, but they are commonly used nonetheless. Personally, I think resumes are somewhat pointless outside of providing a chronology of work history. They are a one-sided, completely biased portrayal written by the applicant themselves where many people stop just short of claiming to cure cancer.

That said, it is SUPPOSED to be perfect, so make sure that it is! There are no excuses here. Use spell-check and get someone who is qualified to proofread it. If you don't know how to abbreviate, ask someone. I'm pretty sure that you've never been an "Ass. Manager," but even if you have, that's not a position here.

> ## "IT IS SUPPOSED TO BE PERFECT, SO MAKE SURE THAT IT IS"

1. WHO DO I KNOW THAT IS QUALIFIED TO PROOFREAD MY RESUME TO ENSURE THAT IT IS FREE OF ANY TYPOS, MISSPELLINGS OR OTHER GRAMMATICAL ERRORS?

_____

_____

_____

— 13 —
IF YOU DON'T HAVE A RESUME, WRITE A COMPELLING COVER LETTER INSTEAD

While I may be skeptical about your resume accomplishments, I am very receptive to hearing about your attributes, character and work ethic.

One or two paragraphs telling me that you are hardworking, honest, responsible, reliable, etc. will often compel me to want to talk with you further. Awards, supplementary education and special skills like speaking other languages are also excellent things to include.

Express your desire to work and that you will make the most of the opportunity. Customizing it by company name will make it more personal and less like a form letter, for example, "I would love the opportunity to work at Bob's Burger Barn, and if given the chance, I promise to give my very best effort."

Never underestimate the power of small beginnings. I had a paper route for three years starting when I was thirteen. I kept that on my resume until I was thirty and still use it as a potential talking point in an interview. It is a foundation that gives insight and depth to my work ethic. Used properly, this can be a very powerful tool.

So, tell me about your paper route, baby sitting or volunteer work that shows me how you were raised and that you are ready to step up into a formal paycheck job. I want to know this because I'm not interested in hiring an adult or even a near adult who has no structural foundation in responsibility or customer service.

> # "NEVER UNDERESTIMATE THE POWER OF SMALL BEGINNINGS"

1. WHAT CAN I WRITE ABOUT MYSELF THAT MIGHT COMPEL AN EMPLOYER TO GRANT ME AN INTERVIEW?

_____

_____

_____

14

I DON'T HIRE RESUMES OR APPLICATIONS. I LOOK FOR WHO YOU ARE, NOT WHAT YOU SAY ABOUT YOURSELF

What you put on paper should not contradict who you are in person. Show me your genuine self. Be polished, but not fake. I'm looking for good character, integrity and a sense of responsibility. Demonstrate those things to me and you have a good shot at getting the job. If you have character, I'll teach you the skills that you need for the job.

> ## "SHOW ME YOUR GENUINE SELF. BE POLISHED, BUT NOT FAKE"

1. HAVE I BEEN HONEST IN MY SELF-PORTRAYAL? IS IT CONSISTENT WITH WHO I REALLY AM?

_____

_____

_____

2. WHAT ARE MY BEST, GENUINE QUALITIES?

_____

_____

——— 15 ———
EVERYTHING IS A TEST - EVERYTHING!

At work, I have a little thing I call "Todd's life lessons." On days when business is slow, I will sometimes teach my employees a lesson that will serve them for a lifetime. This is one of those.

If you will simply consider the possibility that everything in life is a test of some kind, you will automatically be better prepared for whatever comes your way. If the sign says "apply before noon," guess what? That's a test. Don't show up at 12:15. If you do show up later, then you should open with: "I know the sign said to come before noon, but I came as soon as I could because of…". Now I know that you read and understood the sign.

About half of my applicants fail this test and demonstrate that they can't follow simple instructions. So, pay attention to the details, because EVERYTHING is a test and there is no prize for second place.

> **"IF YOU WILL SIMPLY CONSIDER THE POSSIBILITY THAT EVERYTHING IN LIFE IS A TEST OF SOME KIND, YOU WILL AUTOMATICALLY BE BETTER PREPARED FOR WHATEVER COMES YOUR WAY"**

1. WHAT THINGS MIGHT AN EMPLOYER VIEW AS A TEST OF MY CHARACTER, SKILL AND WORK ETHIC?

_____

_____

_____

2. WHAT CAN I DO TO PREPARE FOR THESE TESTS?

_____

_____

16

PUNCTUALITY IS PARAMOUNT

If you can't be on time, you can't work for me and there is a fair chance that we can't be friends either.

Few things irritate me more than tardiness. It is rampant in society and business everywhere. I've known doctors who justify their inability to be on time almost to the point of bragging about it - "professionals" not being professional. The fact that it is commonplace should by no means imply that it is okay, because it is not!

Punctuality means on time. Never late - but also, not too early. I recommend being no more than 10 minutes early. Any more than that and I start to think that you can't tell time or can't follow instructions. If I wanted you here earlier, I would have said so.

Habitual tardiness shows that you are unorganized, self-centered and self-indulgent; lacking courtesy and respect for others. Too harsh? Too bad. That's as nice as I get on the subject; especially, when it comes to employees…and doctors.

> ## "PUNCTUALITY MEANS ON TIME. HABITUAL TARDINESS SHOWS THAT YOU ARE UNORGANIZED…"

1. AM I CONSISTENTLY PUNCTUAL? IF NOT, WHAT STEPS AND ACTIONS WILL I TAKE TO BECOME MORE RELIABLE?

_____

_____

_____

— 17 —

A GOOD, FIRM HANDSHAKE SPEAKS VOLUMES - SO DOES A WEAK, SQUISHY ONE

There are some things that I don't fully understand nor can I fully explain. This is one of them, and I know that I'm not alone. Whether you are a man, woman or young adult, you need to learn how to properly shake hands.

It's not a competition of strength and if you crush my hand I'm not going to be pleased. But, if you wiggle a cold, clammy, dead fish in my hand, I'm going to have a hard time focusing on anything else about you.

If you look me in the eye, shake my hand with a firm grip, a dry hand and a sense of confidence, then you will be off to a great start!

"YOU NEED TO LEARN HOW TO PROPERLY SHAKE HANDS"

1. DO I HAVE A GOOD, FIRM HANDSHAKE?

_____

_____

_____

2. DO I LOOK PEOPLE IN THE EYE WHEN I SHAKE THEIR HAND?

_____

_____

_____

— 18 —

I'M HIRING BASED ON MY NEEDS. YOUR NEEDS ARE NOT A MAJOR FACTOR FOR ME

I knew that you needed a job the moment that you applied, so telling me that you REALLY need a job is redundant and it's not a compelling reason for me to hire you. You shouldn't lead with it when asked the "Why do you want to work here?" question.

Sometimes, people come across as desperate. Too many personal and/ or financial problems may be viewed as a red flag and fairly or not, cause speculation as to why you can't get or keep a job. "I really want to work here" is much better than "I really need a job" and be sure to have a couple of answers ready when they ask you "why?"

You need to tell me what you can do for me. I'm looking for someone to solve my problems, and I'm willing to pay somebody to do it. If you can convey to me that you are that person, then we are both going to get what we want.

> ## "'I REALLY WANT TO WORK HERE' IS MUCH BETTER THAN 'I REALLY NEED A JOB'"

1. HOW CAN I ANSWER QUESTIONS IN A WAY THAT WILL DEMONSTRATE AN INTEREST IN THE EMPLOYER'S NEEDS ABOVE MY OWN?

_____

_____

_____

2. HOW CAN I CONVEY A DESIRE TO SERVE RATHER THAN A NEED TO BE SERVED?

_____

_____

— 19 —
WHAT ARE YOU THAT WOULD MAKE ME STUPID NOT TO HIRE YOU

Are you smart, honest, hard-working, fast-learning, reliable, punctual, loyal, friendly? The list goes on. If you can make a solid impression that reveals your best qualities, then your value as a candidate will rise. You may only have seconds to convey that message, so lead with your best.

> "YOU MAY ONLY HAVE SECONDS TO CONVEY THAT MESSAGE, SO LEAD WITH YOUR BEST"

1. WHAT ARE MY TOP THREE QUALITIES THAT MAY BE BENEFICIAL TO MY EMPLOYER?

_____

_____

_____

2. HOW WILL I GET THOSE POINTS ACROSS WHEN MAKING MY FIRST IMPRESSIONS?

_____

_____

_____

— 20 —

WHEN YOU'RE WAITING IN THE LOBBY FOR AN APPOINTMENT OR INTERVIEW, STAY OFF YOUR PHONE. IT IMPLIES THAT SOMETHING ELSE IS MORE IMPORTANT

I'm very punctual. So, if you show up early to meet with me, you are most likely going to wait right up to the scheduled time. I can't tell you how many times I have approached an applicant right on time only to have to wait for them to conclude whatever business they are conducting on their phone.

I have also stepped away for a moment to get a form or something else relevant to the meeting only to find them on the phone again! Making me compete for your attention may be that bad second or third impression that I mentioned earlier that utterly wipes out your good first impression.

This is more than just bad manners. You have unwittingly put your job opportunity in jeopardy. It may not be a death blow, but then again, it might be. You really need to focus on the idea that you are trying to get me to give you a job - everything else can wait!

> **"MAKING ME COMPETE FOR YOUR ATTENTION MAY BE THAT BAD SECOND IMPRESSION THAT UTTERLY WIPES OUT YOUR GOOD FIRST IMPRESSION"**

1. WHAT THINGS CAN I DO TO ENSURE THAT I REMAIN FOCUSED AT EVERY STAGE OF THE APPLICATION AND INTERVIEW PROCESS?

_____

_____

_____

2. SHOULD I SILENCE MY PHONE, TURN IT OFF OR JUST LEAVE IT IN THE CAR?

_____

_____

— 21 —

EVERYONE HAS MANNERS - GOOD OR BAD. MAKE SURE THAT ONLY YOUR BEST ARE ON DISPLAY

These days good manners and etiquette are dying virtues. Too many people are too self-absorbed and oblivious to others. It's such a shame. Good manners are extremely valuable!

Sitting up straight, making eye contact and paying attention shows respect for others. Using words like, please, thank you, pardon me, sir and ma'am will separate you from the pack - not only in the job hunt, but in all of life.

> "USING WORDS LIKE, PLEASE, THANK YOU, PARDON ME, SIR AND MA'AM WILL SEPARATE YOU FROM THE PACK."

1. WHAT GOOD MANNERS SHOULD I ACTIVELY DISPLAY IN THE PRESENCE OF MY PROSPECTIVE EMPLOYER?

_____

_____

_____

2. WHAT BAD MANNERS SHOULD I AVOID AT ALL COST?

_____

_____

22

YOUR BODY LANGUAGE IS SO LOUD THAT I CAN'T HEAR WHAT YOUR MOUTH IS SAYING

Do you lean or slouch? Have nervous tics? Do you roll your eyes or curl your lips? Are you doodling, spinning your pen or picking your fingernails while we talk? Do you look bored or uninterested? Are you staring out the window distracted or daydreaming? I've seen it all…and then some!

You really need to pay attention to your body language, because I can assure you that your prospective employer is watching and taking notes.

"YOU REALLY NEED TO PAY ATTENTION TO YOUR BODY LANGUAGE"

1. WHAT NON-VERBAL COMMUNICATION AM I AWARE OF THAT I SHOULD BE MINDFUL OF WHEN APPLYING OR INTERVIEWING FOR A JOB?

_____

_____

_____

2. DO I PAY ATTENTION TO MY BODY LANGUAGE SO THAT I DON'T INADVERTENTLY SEND THE WRONG MESSAGE?

_____

_____

23

HAVE YOU HELD A JOB FOR MORE THAN A YEAR OR HAVE YOU HAD SIX JOBS LASTING ONE TO THREE MONTHS?

Job history says a lot about you. Unless it is seasonal or temporary work, tenure of less than six months is a red flag and going to be viewed as a negative. I don't care what they told you, but McDonalds doesn't "lay-off" cooks and cashiers and putting that on your application tells me that you probably got fired – sorry to have be the one to tell you.

You should also avoid using terms like: "quit", "terminated", "fired", etc. These things suggest that you are, and will be a problem employee, and I'm going to take a hard pass. It's better to just leave it off the application and avoid mentioning it at all if possible.

If you did leave after a short term, and you really were a good employee, ask for a letter of recommendation and make plenty of copies! I love giving letters to good employees, and I love receiving them from applicants. Letters of recommendation from teachers, pastors and volunteer organizations are also a great way to distinguish yourself.

> ## "I LOVE GIVING LETTERS TO GOOD EMPLOYEES, AND I LOVE RECEIVING THEM FROM APPLICANTS"

1. DOES MY RESUME SHOW THAT I HAVE A LOT OF EXPERIENCE OR IMPLY THAT I CAN'T KEEP A JOB?

_____

_____

_____

2. ARE THERE POTENTIAL "RED FLAGS" LIKE SHORT TERMS OF EMPLOYMENT OR BIG TIME GAPS BETWEEN JOBS? SHOULD I ADDRESS THIS UP FRONT AND AM I PREPARED TO EXPLAIN ANY ISSUES?

_____

_____

_____

24

AVOID USING ANY AND ALL PROFANITY

This is one of those things that I shouldn't have to say, but it is not uncommon for applicants to use vulgar language and profanity at various times in the process of applying or even in the interview.

Nobody is dropping F-bombs, but I've heard just about everything else. If you're just not paying attention to yourself, then snap out of it! If you think that this somehow makes you appear cool and hip, well, you're wrong, and I will not hire you or your foul mouth. To assume familiarity in a formal setting is not being friendly, it is presumptuous.

If you do manage to get the job, avoid profanity in the workplace, too. It pollutes the environment and makes work unpleasant for others whether they tell you or not. Pretend that you're in church or court or at your grandma's house. You have the ability to set a higher standard, so do it.

"TO ASSUME FAMILIARITY IN A FORMAL SETTING IS NOT BEING FRIENDLY, IT IS PRESUMPTUOUS"

1. AM I MINDFUL, RESPECTFUL AND INTENTIONAL IN THE WORDS I USE?

_____

_____

_____

2. HOW HIGH IS THE STANDARD OF CONDUCT THAT I HAVE SET FOR MYSELF?

_____

_____

_____

25

HAVING NO QUESTIONS IMPLIES A LACK OF THOUGHT, PREPARATION AND INTEREST

Having no questions is almost as bad as asking the wrong ones. Avoid questions that are self-serving like: "How much does it pay?" "Can I have weekends off?" "When do I get a raise?" If it sounds like "me, me, me", you should re-think it. There will be time to discuss things like that later.

Right now, you're trying to get the job, so ask questions that benefit the employer. Things like, "In addition to my cashier duties, what other duties will I be doing?" This shows that you are willing to do more than just handle cash. Now, when they answer you, you can respond with an enthusiastic "I can do that!"

Other questions like: "How many people are you hiring for this position?" and "What are the most important qualifications for this position?". This may seem a little self-serving, but it demonstrates that you are thinking in terms of their needs and are willing to conform to those requirements.

"RIGHT NOW, YOU'RE TRYING TO GET THE JOB, SO ASK QUESTIONS THAT BENEFIT THE EMPLOYER"

1. WHAT ARE THREE QUESTIONS THAT I CAN BE PREPARED TO ASK?

_____

_____

_____

— 26 —

IF YOU ARE NOT MAKING EYE CONTACT, YOU ARE TALKING NEAR ME, NOT WITH ME

Eye contact is key to good communication. It says that you are present, focused and paying attention. It's also another of those good manners that I've mentioned. But, don't overdo it. A good rule to remember is: "Eye contact good - staring, bad!"

Also, remember that when you are talking, I need to understand you, so speak loud enough and clearly. Avoid using language and jargon that is too casual. Say "yes" and "no", not "yeah" and "nah". And unless you're talking about a ranch where you once worked, the word "dude" in any context may be the end of the interview – especially if you are referring to me!

> ## "A GOOD RULE TO REMEMBER IS: 'EYE CONTACT GOOD - STARING, BAD!'"

1. AM I GOOD AT MAKING EYE CONTACT? IF NOT, WHAT STEPS CAN I TAKE TO IMPROVE?

_____

_____

_____

—— 27 ——

ENTRY LEVEL JOBS ARE DIFFERENT FROM CAREER JOBS SO CONDUCT YOURSELF ACCORDINGLY. YOU MAY LOOK SHARP IN YOUR THREE-PIECE SUIT, BUT IF YOU'RE APPLYING TO FLIP BURGERS AND SCOOP FRIES, YOU MAY BE OVERDRESSED

My wife hates this tip and disagrees - easy to do from the sidelines. "Dress for success" has its place, but it is not here. In the real world, I'm telling you that trying too hard is going to have a negative result. If you dress like a banker, I may think that you won't want to do the blue-collar job that I'm hiring for. Be yourself. Be the best version of you, but, don't overshoot your target.

> **"BE YOURSELF. BE THE BEST VERSION OF YOU, BUT, DON'T OVERSHOOT YOUR TARGET"**

1. WHAT ATTIRE WOULD BE APPROPRIATE FOR THE JOB I'M APPLYING FOR?

_____

_____

_____

2. WHAT SHOULD I NOT WEAR?

_____

_____

_____

— 28 —

EVERYONE HAS A WEBSITE. LEARN A LITTLE BIT ABOUT THE BUSINESS BEFORE YOU APPLY

The "about us" tab on the company website is a cookie jar full of goodies for the job seeker who wants an edge over the competition.

Too many job seekers are broadcasting their efforts over too many places and getting zero traction. Pick a few places where you honestly think you would like to work and focus on those places. If it doesn't produce a job, then add a few more and keep going.

By learning a little bit about a company, you are arming yourself with knowledge that may be invaluable in your job search. Where did they start? How many years have they been in business? What's their mission statement? How many locations do they have? All of this information, and more, is there for the taking and just knowing some of it will separate you from the pack, so, do it!

> **"BY LEARNING A LITTLE BIT ABOUT A COMPANY, YOU ARE ARMING YOURSELF WITH KNOWLEDGE"**

1. WHAT ARE THREE THINGS THAT I HAVE LEARNED ABOUT THE COMPANY I'M APPLYING AT?

_____

_____

_____

29

SOME HIRING MANAGERS SUCK AT INTERVIEWING

This one's not your fault. There are countless managers who may be great in every other area of their jobs except for the hiring process. Unfortunately, they still hold the keys to the kingdom, so if you really want the job, you are going to have to navigate your way through their inadequacies.

Pay attention, ask the right questions and try to adapt to their style. They're still looking for the best candidates so don't get distracted by their mannerisms. Work through it with confidence and you may be rewarded with the job.

"PAY ATTENTION, ASK THE RIGHT QUESTIONS AND TRY TO ADAPT TO THEIR STYLE"

1. HOW CAN I MAKE THINGS EASIER FOR THE PERSON INTERVIEWING ME?

_____

_____

_____

—— 30 ——
YOU ARE SELLING YOURSELF

There's an old adage that says everyone is a salesman. There's a lot of truth in that. In this case, your ability to sell yourself to an employer is the "price" of getting a job.

When I was in sales, I was taught that a "feature" is what something does and a "benefit" is what it does for you. Always sell benefits.
Maybe your features are "punctual and reliable." So, your benefits are that you can be trusted to arrive for early morning shifts and require little supervision.

Selling yourself to a potential employer by highlighting not only what you can do, but specifically, what you can do for them will quickly move you in the right direction.

"YOUR ABILITY TO SELL YOURSELF TO AN EMPLOYER IS THE "PRICE" OF GETTING A JOB"

1. WHAT SKILLS, ATTRIBUTES OR QUALITIES DO YOU HAVE THAT CAN BE FRAMED AS A BENEFIT TO AN EMPLOYER? HOW CAN YOU INTERJECT THAT IN AN INTERVIEW?

_____

_____

_____

— 31 —
SMALL DETAILS ARE OFTEN THE MOST IMPORTANT ONES

In my introduction, I mentioned self-sabotage. The biggest obstacle to getting a job just might be YOU! In fact, it is.

Smokey the Bear says that "Only YOU can prevent forest fires!" It is equally true that only YOU can win or lose a job opportunity.

Sure, there are a lot of things that you can blame. People do it all the time. But, if a job is available, and you know that you meet the requirements, then 99% of the time the results lie in what you did or did not do. It may be an oversimplification, but truth is simple.

You need to pay attention to the details and no detail is too small. Using pink ink and dotting your "i's" with little hearts makes me think that you are too immature for the job. Poof! Opportunity dead. Unfair? Maybe - but you're trying to get a job where I give you money and trust you with my business, so once again, get your head in the game!

> ## "YOU NEED TO PAY ATTENTION TO THE DETAILS AND NO DETAIL IS TOO SMALL"

1. LOOKING THROUGH AN EMPLOYER'S EYES, WHAT DETAILS MAY BE HURTING MY CHANCES OF GETTING THE JOB? WHAT CORRECTIVE ACTIONS SHOULD I TAKE?

_____

_____

_____

—— BONUS LESSON ——
THE INTERVIEW

I originally didn't intend to address the face-to-face interview. The reason being, if you have done the things in the book and got the interview, then, you are already primed to ace the interview! The bonus lesson here is more of a pep-talk to help you realize that fact and hopefully give you a little boost in your confidence. You've done all the right things up to this point, but here are a few things to consider so that you don't drop the ball at the very end.

Think of the interview as a first date. You're properly dressed, groomed and on time. Being a little nervous/excited is expected and actually a positive thing. Nervous/scared/intimidated is a negative; so, think it through, but don't obsess. They already liked you enough to ask you for the "date," now you just need to get to know each other a little bit.

Be polite and friendly, but also, a little reserved with decorum (a great word for you to look up in the dictionary!) Your interviewer wants to know a little more about you and may make some casual conversation about school, family, hobbies, favorite movies or other things, so be prepared to discuss any appropriate subjects about yourself that may be completely unrelated to the job. This is normal, in fact, it's a good sign when an employer wants to know a little bit about your personal life. It's an indication that they see you as a person and not a thing. The more places you work, the more you will understand the value of this - trust me.

Now, to the nitty-gritty. They want to know if you meet the specific requirements of the job. This will involve questions about basic skill sets and requirements, learning or physical limitations/disabilities, schedule availability, transportation and other variables that may impact work in the short or long term. For example; a 2-week class trip to Europe in December may be an issue if I'm hiring for Christmas help. A planned family vacation in the summer may also be good to know. Be honest about these things - even if it's a deal-breaker. You don't have to disclose every little thing, but springing "surprises" after the fact and expecting your employer to acquiesce is presumptuous and might well get you fired, so beware.

They may also want to know how long you plan to stick around. For me, I prefer a year or longer, but I want someone for at least six months to make it worth my time and effort. This will be different for all employers and in college towns, they understand the school dynamic; but it often takes weeks or longer for new employees to be trained and fully productive and no employer wants to be continually hiring every few months because of your short-term plans.

Don't wait to be asked every question. You should be having a comfortable, semi-casual conversation and this is a great time to mention special skills and talents like, speaking other languages or a relevant award or achievement. These are extra things that make you stand out and shine. Have a few questions for your interviewer. They can be job related, but don't be afraid to step a little outside the box. If you're a college student, you might ask how many other college students are working there and what they like most about the job. Ask about career and advancement opportunities that may be available and if the company has plans to expand in the area. Ask the interviewer how long they have worked for the company and what they like about it. People like to talk about themselves - even bosses! Be respectful and don't overstep the bounds of professional etiquette, but don't be afraid to talk to them like a real person, it shows that you're engaging and interested in others.

Finally, remember that this is in fact a first or second entry-level job. Future higher-level jobs will require higher levels of job-seeking and interviewing skills than what I've offered here, but this will get you this job now and that's the purpose. There are things and people that you will both love and hate. I've had some horrible jobs, bosses, co-workers and customers in my early years, but it is the fabric of life and I wouldn't change a thing; so, keep the perspective that you're embarking on an adventure. Congratulations! I think you just got hired!

" CONGRATULATIONS! I THINK YOU JUST GOT HIRED!"

FINAL THOUGHTS...

There you have it - a short list of things to think about, things to do and things to avoid. Challenge yourself to implement as many of these things as you can in your job search. Evaluate yourself every chance you get and make course corrections along the way. Use your resources. Use people who can help you.

I've written this as a workbook of practical, effective tips, advice and observations that is easy to read, easy to understand and easy to implement. It was born out of personal frustration from what I see every day in the workplace. People who may be very qualified to do the actual job, but disqualify themselves because they are oblivious to what should be obvious. I want to help those people.

Make a commitment to excellence in everything that you do. Work on your presentation skills. Get a teacher or a parent or youth pastor to role-play with you. They'll be happy that you asked! Have someone make a video of you greeting, shaking hands, introducing yourself and asking for an application. Do a short, mock interview. Then, watch it over and over again looking for ways to improve.

If you will do these things, I truly believe that you will get the job faster and easier than any of your friends and see greater success in your life. It's not the things that you can't do that are hurting you, it's the things that you can do, but don't. Nothing I've written here is complicated or difficult. For whatever reasons though, most people simply don't do these things.

I hope there are some "Wow!" moments where a light bulb went off in your head and that this provides you with some confidence and direction not only in your job search, but in all of life. Thank you for reading. I hope this serves you well as you step up into your future!

NOW GO BACK NOW AND ANSWER THE "FIRST IMPRESSION" QUESTION AT THE BEGINNING OF THE BOOK.

If you purchased this book from Amazon, please rate it and post a short review and if this book has helped you or someone you know, I'd love to hear from you. Questions, comments and booking inquiries can be sent to *themanagerwhisperer @gmail.com*